2003

the Jack Russell Terrier

A Comprehensive Guide to Buying, Owning and Training

by Alan and Maureen Broadstock

Willow Creek Press

MINOCQUA, WISCONSIN

ABOUT THE AUTHORS

Alan and Maureen Broadstock established their Arad kennel more than 20 years ago, and they have an international reputation as terrier experts. They have kept Staffordshire Bull Terriers for many years, but now specialise in the Parson Russell Terrier. Alan has a particular interest in the history of the breed, and he has an unparalleled collection of memorabilia which includes books, paintings, and porcelain.

Alan and Maureen are both Championship show judges, and have travelled around the world on judging appointments. Maureen is currently Treasurer of the Parson Russell Terrier Club – a position she has held for nine years. She has recently had the great honour of being made a member of the Kennel Club.

ACKNOWLEDGEMENTS

The publisher would like to thank the following for help with photography: Wendy and Steve Houtz (Thistle Ridge Jack Russells), June Golden, Cheryl Libby, Kathy Pobloskie (Just Say Go Flyball Team), Patricia Cranmer (Fox Shadow Jack Russells), Ken Bushell (Natural Instinct Jack Russell Terriers), Lyn Rock and Les Price (Otherton), Sue and Vic Reeks, and Jo Sollis. Page 66: Irish Ch. Jackmass Titania of Jagen. Page 80: Helbeck Izzi-rite for Jagen, top winning dog in UK, owned by Rock and Price of Otherton Kennels.

VETERINARY CONTRIBUTION

Viv Alemi (author of Chapter Seven: Health Care) graduated from the Royal (Dick) School of Veterinary Studies, Edinburgh, in 1996. He went on to work in a large practice, where he treated pets of all types and also did a small amount of farm work. In 2002, Viv, together with two colleagues, took over a veterinary practice in Royal Leamington Spa, Warwickshire, UK.

Throughout the text, the Jack Russell Terrier has been referred to as 'he' instead of 'it' – but no gender bias is intended.

Printed and bound in Taiwan by Sino
Library of Congress Cataloging-in-Publication Data

Broadstock, Alan.
 The Jack Russell terrier : a comprehensive guide to buying, owning, and training / by Alan and Maureen Broadstock.
   p. cm. -- (Breed basics)
 ISBN 1-57223-511-X (hardcover)
 1. Jack Russell terrier. I. Broadstock, Maureen. II. Title. III Series.
 SF429.J27 B755 2002
 636.755--dc21

                                              2002002625

Contents

What Makes A Russell Special?

Every breed has its enthusiasts, but the Jack Russell Terrier (known in the UK as the Parson Russell Terrier) is not content with the faithful few. He has a huge international fan club, who are all passionate about this little dog from the West Country. What is it that makes the Russell so special?

THE RUSSELL MIND

There are many reasons why an individual may be attracted to a particular breed. It may be the coat, the colour or the markings, or the size may be suitable for a particular lifestyle, but the most important factor is character. Hopefully, you will share your life with your dog for a decade or more, so it is essential to find a compatible partner!

The Russell is bold and friendly. He has an extrovert, outgoing approach to life, and this is reflected in his dealings with everyone he meets. Nervousness is completely contrary to the spirit of the Russell. Bred as a working dog, going to ground after fox, he had to be fearless, and this tough, courageous attitude remains a hallmark of the breed. However, this does not mean that the Russell is aggressive.

His job was to go underground and bolt the fox, or to hold it at bay until the huntsmen arrived. He had to be determined, and able to stand his ground, but he was not required to attack.

At home, the Russell is lively and playful. He loves a game, and seems to come alive when he is given a job to do. The alert, inquisitive expression on his face as he retrieves a toy, or finds a hidden treat, sums up his bright, intelligent nature. Although the Russell was not bred as a guard dog, he will be aware of all the comings and goings in your house and in the immediate neighbourhood. If a visitor is approaching, or a cat is in the garden, your Russell will be the first to tell you!

Lively and playful, the Russell thrives on being the centre of attention.

The tough side of the Russell is balanced with an unexpected sweetness. He is a loving member of the family, and can be extremely affectionate. He is good with children, although it is important that both children and dog are taught a sense of mutual respect (see page 34). In terms of trainability, there is no doubting the Russell's brain power, but, like many of the terrier breeds, he retains a certain degree of independence. He enjoys being the centre of attention, but he has no desire to be mollycoddled.

A sensible, no-nonsense breed, the Russell offers wonderful companionship, as well as great entertainment. He fills the gap in your life – and once you have owned a Russell, no other breed will do.

PHYSICAL CHARACTERISTICS

The Russell is a handy-sized dog, measuring around 13 in (33 cm) at the shoulder. The male should be slightly bigger, ideally reaching 14 in (35 cm). He is built on workmanlike lines, without any exaggeration. He is active and agile, and can run for miles without tiring. This is an important consideration to bear in mind if you are thinking of taking on a Russell. The breed may be small in size, but an adult dog will need plenty of exercise.

The coat may be smooth, which is very easy to care for, or it may be rough- or broken-coated. This type of coat requires routine grooming, but it also needs to be stripped at least twice a year (see pages 69-72). The predominant colour is white, with black, lemon or tan markings. In the show ring, it is preferred if markings are confined to the head and the root of the tail, but this is not important for the companion dog.

Developed on workmanlike lines, this is a breed without exaggeration.

Traditionally, the tail was always docked. For the working terrier, the stipulation was that the length of the tail complemented the body, and also provided a good handhold. Today, docking is banned in some countries, although the breed is still exhibited in the show ring with a docked tail in both the UK and the USA.

WHERE DO THEY COME FROM?

Tracing the history of dog breeds is not an exact science, and often legend and anecdote have to be relied upon rather than discovering concrete facts. However, the Russell historian has no such problems. This is a breed that was invented by one person – the Reverend John Russell – and the breed carries his name to this day.

John Russell, a passionate foxhunter, had a vision of the ideal working terrier. He devoted his life to developing a breed that was perfectly suited to the task of keeping pace with horses all day, and then going to ground after fox. He had a very clear idea of the temperament that was required, and the physical characteristics needed to do the job, and his findings were well documented. Breeders today are in the unique position of having a precise picture of the Russell, handed down by the man who invented the breed.

THE FIRST RUSSELL

John Russell was born in Dartmouth, in Devon, England in 1795. At the age of 13 years, he attended Blundell's School in Tiverton, and it was there that the young John discovered a passion for hunting. With a fellow pupil, he set up a pack of foxhounds, but, all too soon, this was discovered by his headmaster. His friend was expelled, and Russell suffered a severe beating.

This did not quash his enthusiasm, and, when he was at university in Oxford, he used every opportunity to go hunting. If funds permitted, he would go hunting four or five days a week, which could have left little time for study! It was in his last year at university

The Rev. John Russell: A man with a passion for hunting. Note the small terrier in the foreground.

that he acquired a terrier bitch, called Trump, who was to be the foundation of the Russell breed.

Russell's friend and biographer, E.W.L. Davies, describes the scene:

"Before he had reached Marston, a milkman met him with a terrier – such an animal as Russell had yet only seen in his dreams; he halted as Actaeon might have done when he caught sight of Diana disporting in her bath; but unlike that ill-fated hunter, he never budged from the spot till he had won the prize and secured it for his own."

A portrait of Trump was painted in 1820, a few months after Russell acquired her. It shows a small white dog, with dark tan markings on her head and at the base of her tail. Her coat appears thick and wiry, and she has the alert, inquisitive expression that is so typical of the breed today. John Russell considered her the ideal terrier, saying: "Her whole appearance gave indications of courage, endurance and hardihood." As Russell went on to develop his own breeding programme, it was this feisty, determined character that he was dedicated to preserve.

DEVELOPING THE BREED

John Russell was ordained in 1819, and was given a parish in South Molton, Devon to look after. He worked hard, but he always found time for hunting. He gathered together a small pack of hounds, and hunted otter in the summer and fox in the winter.

In 1826, he married Penelope Bury and they moved to Iddlesleigh. The work was less demanding in this parish, and soon Russell was able to enlarge his pack of hounds and concentrate on foxhunting. The terrain was tough, and the dogs had to keep pace with huntsmen on horseback throughout a long, hard day. Russell therefore bred for speed and stamina, as well as for the courageous temperament that he considered so essential. It was reported that Trump, and her descendant Tip, could run a gruelling 15-20 miles on a hunt.

In 1833, the Russells moved to Swimbridge, and this was to be their home for the next 45 years. Russell served his parishioners well, but foxhunting remained his great passion. The fame of his terriers spread outside Devon, and many of his dogs were bought as foundation stock for other packs. "Where shall you find any terrier strain, or for that matter any strain of dogs, so honoured and renowned as that of the Devonshire Parson?" asked an admiring contemporary.

We are fortunate in having a number of written descriptions of Parson Russell's terriers. Thomas Henry Pearce, writing in *The Dog* in 1872, gave the following picture in words:

"The peculiar texture [of the coat] does not interfere with the profile of the body, though there is a shaggy eyebrow and a pronounced moustache. The eyebrows are the great mark, giving the dog the look of a Bristol merchant. Mr Russell's [dogs] have a keen jaw; narrow but strong; short, well-set limbs; a long back; small ears; and white is the prevailing colour; a hard-coated enduring dog, fit for any work, however hard, with a rough jacket, defiant of all weather, and resolution (combined with sense enough) to serve him in all difficulties."

John Russell's wife, Penelope, with one of the Parson's terriers.

THE LEGACY

Russell died in 1883, and his few remaining dogs were taken on by friends and hunt colleagues. However, the breed he had developed did not die out. Several breeders, such as Miss Serrell and Augusta Guest bred terriers on similar lines as did Russell.

Then came Arthur Heinemann, who worked tirelessly to keep the breed alive after the Parson's death. He became the secretary of the Parson Jack Russell Club, and was instrumental in writing a Breed Standard based on the terriers that Russell had bred.

It seemed as though the breed's future was assured, but, in the years following the Second World War, the Jack Russell faced major upheavals. Like many breeds, the number of Russell Terriers dwindled during the war years, but when peace was restored there

*The Parson's terrier was crossed with other breeds,
and a new, short-legged terrier gained popularity.*

was a new threat. There was a move to cross the Russell with other breeds, and these ranged from the Chihuahua and the Corgi to various terrier breeds, including the Lakeland, the Fox Terrier and the Staffordshire Bull Terrier. A new type of short-legged terrier emerged, which became very popular as a family dog. But, as there was no control over breeding, there was no uniformity of type, and it seemed as though the breed created by Parson Russell would be lost forever.

However, a group of enthusiasts, based in Devon, continued to breed dogs that were true to the original type, and, after a long struggle, the breed was recognised by the English Kennel Club. Today it is known as the Parson Russell Terrier, and breeders are dedicated to preserving the Parson's terrier, as described by Heinemann in his Breed Standard, which has become the basis for the Standard adopted by the Kennel Club.

TRANSATLANTIC LINKS

The Russell now has a worldwide following, and is particularly popular in the USA and in Australia. It is interesting to note that, in Australia, both the short-legged Jack Russell and the long-legged Parson type, have official recognition.

The little terrier from the West Country quickly found fame in the USA. To begin with, breeding was fairly indiscriminate, but dedicated breeders soon started to import dogs of the true Parson type from the UK. This has given the breed a strong foundation in its new home, and the quality and temperament of dogs in the US is now first-class.

To confuse the issue, a copyright was placed on the name Parson Jack Russell in the US, which means that this name cannot be used for the breed. It is therefore known as the Jack Russell Terrier, but it remains true in type to the Parson's terrier.

THE RUSSELL TODAY

The Russell was bred as a working terrier, and the breed retains a strong working instinct. Indeed, many of the breed are still used for hunting where legislation permits. In the UK, the Russell is still used to go to ground after fox. He can bolt the fox so the hunt can continue on its trail, or he can bark to alert the terrierman as to the quarry's location. Other legal quarry in the UK includes rabbits, rats and mink. In the USA, legal quarry varies from state to state, but groundhog and possum are the most common.

The Russell is still used for hunting in some areas.

Even if you have no wish to work your terrier in the traditional way, there is still an opportunity to test his skills. Many Russells compete in Earth Dog events, organised by the American Kennel Club, and show great enthusiasm for the sport (see pages 86-87). The Russell is also highly valued as a 'stable terrier' living alongside horses, and keeping the barns free of mice and rats.

Jack Of all Trades

The Russell loves to have his mind occupied, and is bright enough to be trained to an advanced level. His speed and energy make him a natural competitor in Agility, and he will relish the opportunity to take part in terrier racing. Obedience training is not always easy, as the Jack Russell is well known for his independent streak, but a number of dedicated trainers have been surprisingly successful.

You would be forgiven for thinking that the Jack Russell is too small to be used as an assistance dog, but this consideration is unimportant when selecting hearing dogs who work with the deaf. Their job is to alert their owner to everyday sounds, such as the door-bell, the telephone (there are specially adapted telephones for the deaf), the fax machine, the cooker-timer and the smoke alarm. The alert Jack Russell, who loves to be involved in everything that is going on, has proved to be an ideal candidate.

The breed's friendly, outgoing nature has also been put to good use, with many Russells working as therapy dogs, visiting hospitals, homes for the elderly, and special schools.

After a long battle for recognition, the Russell is now making his mark in the show ring.

In the show ring, the Russell cuts a smart figure, and, as the breed becomes more popular, it is increasingly important that the best specimens of the breed are exhibited in the ring and go forward to be used for breeding.

THE PERFECT COMPANION

Adaptable, outgoing, and full of character, the Russell is a breed that can fit in with a variety of different lifestyles. He will enjoy being part of a big family, but he will be just as happy to live with one or two people. He is a fun-loving individual, and he will bring light and laughter into his owner's life. He will enjoy all challenges that come his way, but, at the end of the day, he will give the best gift of all – companionship.

The legacy of John Russell lives on in the shape of the little terrier from the West Country, who is now a worldwide favourite.

Choosing A Russell

It is a well-known fact that all puppies are adorable. It takes a will of iron to resist a beautiful little puppy, and yet the implications of taking on a dog are far-reaching. For this reason, it is essential to weigh up all the pros and cons of dog ownership before you go and see a litter.

MAKING THE DECISION

Start by asking yourself the following questions:

- Are the whole family committed to the idea of taking on a puppy?
- Will there be someone at home most of the day? A dog should not be left on his own for longer than four hours.
- Can you afford to keep a dog? The cost of food, veterinary bills, and boarding kennels should all be taken into consideration.
- Will you be able to care for your dog for the duration of his lifetime?

If you are confident that you can cope with these general requirements, you should then work out whether you have the makings of a Russell owner.

The Russell is an intelligent dog that needs a programme of training.

- Do you have the time to exercise a Russell? This is a breed that requires two or three outings a day.
- Are you prepared to train your Russell? This is an intelligent breed that may get up to mischief if the brain is not occupied.
- Do you understand the Russell mind? This is a working terrier, bred to go to ground. You may well find that your Russell retains this instinct, and will use every opportunity to disappear down the nearest hole!
- Can you afford to take your Russell to a professional groomer? If you choose a rough-coated Russell, the coat will need stripping at least twice a year.

If you, and your family, are still full of enthusiasm for the Russell, the next task is to locate a puppy.

FINDING A BREEDER

Do not be in a rush to go out and buy the first Russell puppy that you see advertised. You are looking for a dog that will be a member of your family for the next twelve years or more, so it is important to find a healthy pup that is typical of the breed, and has a sound temperament.

The best plan is to contact your national kennel club which will have a list of registered breeders. You may be given the details of a breed club secretary, who will be able to put you in touch with breeders in your area that have puppies available.

You can also look through the specialist dog papers, or surf the net to find out what is available. However, you must make sure that you only apply to registered breeders. There are unscrupulous people who breed purely for profit, and the puppies they produce may have been reared in poor circumstances, or they may not even be purebred.

When you first make contact, a responsible breeder will probably give you a thorough grilling before you are invited to visit the kennel. Do not take offence; the breeder is making sure that you are able to provide a suitable home for one of their precious puppies.

PUPPY WATCHING

When you go to see the litter, look out for the following points which indicate that the puppies have been properly reared

- The accommodation, whether it is in the house, or in a kennel, should be clean and airy, and it should smell fresh.
- There should be no sign of excreta. If one of the puppies has an 'accident' it should be cleared up immediately.
- If the puppies have been reared in a kennel environment, check with the breeder to ensure they have been given periods of socialisation in the house (see pages 58-61).
- The puppies should be friendly and inquisitive. They should be keen to come up and greet you.

The puppies
should be
bright and
alert, and
ready to come
up to greet you.

The pups should look well covered, without appearing pot-bellied. The eyes should be bright, and there should be no discharge from the eyes or nose. Any sign of dirt around the rear could indicate diarrhoea.

You should be able to see the mother of the puppies. She may not be looking her best (bitches often shed their coat when they are feeding pups), but she should be bright and lively, and happy to show off her puppies.

In most cases, you will not have the opportunity to see the father of the pups, as he will probably belong to another breeder. However, you should be able to see a photo of him, and you should also be able to meet close relatives of the puppies. This will give you a good indication of how the puppies will turn out in terms of general type and temperament.

You should also check with the breeder that both parents have been tested clear for inherited eye conditions (see pages 107, 111-112).

MALE OR FEMALE?

Some people have a preference for owning a male or a female. In reality, there is not a great deal of difference in character. Both are equally loyal and affectionate. Sometimes a female may be slightly more focused on one member of the family, whereas males tend to be friends with everyone.

If you take on a female, you will have to cope with her seasonal cycle, unless you plan to have her spayed (see page 65). When a bitch comes into season, which occurs roughly every nine months, she must be kept away from males for a three-week period to avoid the risk of a mis-mating.

A male will mark his territory when he becomes sexually mature, and he will also be quick to discover if any bitches are in season in the neighbourhood. Neutering is an option worth considering (see page 65).

If you already have a dog at home, it is advisable to get a pup of the opposite sex. Although this may pose management problems if the dogs are not neutered, they will probably get on better with each other. Russell bitches often get on fine with bitches of other breeds, but they are not so keen on their own kind.

The mother of the puppies should have a sound temperament, and she should be happy to show off her puppies.

COAT AND MARKINGS

If you want to keep grooming to a minimum, choose a smooth-coated puppy. Rough- or broken-coated pups will look a little more whiskery at this stage. As the coat grows, it will require regular stripping by a professional groomer (see pages 71-72).

If you are planning to show your Russell, you will be looking for a pup that is not too heavily marked – preferably markings should be confined to the head and the root of the tail. For the companion dog, it is all a matter of personal preference. Many pet owners like 'odd' markings, such as a patch over one eye, as it all adds to the character of the Jack Russell.

CAREER MOVES

Talk to the breeder about your plans for your Jack Russell, and this will help you to find the pup that is most likely to suit. Be honest about your experience with dogs, and whether you have ambitions to go in for showing, or any other type of competition, as such plans will have a big influence on your choice.

If you are looking for a puppy with show potential, remember the breeder cannot offer any guarantees that the pup will make the grade. Using their experience and expertise, they can point out the pup who is most likely to be successful. In many cases, a breeder will 'run on' a couple of puppies that appear to have show quality to see how they mature. By the time a pup is six or seven months of age, it is usually easier to make a judgement.

If you are planning to compete with your Russell in one of the canine disciplines, look for a bright, lively pup, who seems people-orientated. Try throwing a toy, and see if he runs out to fetch it. Ask if you can take the pup away from his littermates so that you can see how well he responds to you.

You may think that if you are looking for a companion, you can simply choose the pup that most appeals to you. But it would be wise

to listen to the advice of the breeder, who will have had the opportunity to assess the temperaments of all the puppies in the litter. Some breeders carry out temperament tests to work out levels of dominance, sociability, and responsiveness. Using this type of information, the breeder will help you to find the pup who is most likely to fit in with your lifestyle.

AN OLDER DOG

There are some situations when taking on an older dog is a better option than coping with a puppy. This may be true of more elderly owners, or if you have very young children. Sometimes a breeder will have an older dog available for a pet home. This could be because a youngster does not have show quality, or it could be because a bitch is to be retired from breeding. Think carefully before taking this route, as, although you will be avoiding the puppy stage, you will be taking on a dog whose character is already formed.

Unfortunately, there are always a number of Russells that end up in rescue shelters and are in need of rehoming. In many cases, this may be through no fault of their own – ill health and marital break-up are the most common reasons for dogs ending up in rescue. However, there are also a proportion of dogs that need rehoming because their owners have failed to cope with them. Often these dogs can be retrained if the new owner has experience with dogs, and lots of patience. But it is not a good idea to go for this option out of sentimentality. You must be confident that you can help the dog to overcome his problems.

GETTING READY

Generally, breeders allow the puppies to go to their new homes at around eight weeks of age. Before your pup is ready to collect, you can use the time to buy the equipment he will need, and you can get to work puppy-proofing your home and garden.

An indoor crate will prove to be a wise investment.

INDOOR CRATE

This is a purchase you will not regret. A crate (also known as a cage) provides safe and secure accommodation for your pup, and can be used at night and at intervals during the day when you cannot supervise him. The crate can be folded up, so it can be used in the car, and it is invaluable if you need to take your pup away from home for a couple of days. The minimum size of crate that will be big enough to accommodate an adult Russell is 24 x 19$^1/_2$ x 22 in (60 x 49 x 55 cm). For information on crate training, see pages 40-41.

You will also need to buy some comfortable bedding to line the crate. The best type is the synthetic fleece fabric which is available in most pet stores. This is machine-washable, and is easy to dry.

OTHER TYPES OF BED

There are lots of different types of dog bed – and some are more practical than others. Strictly speaking, you do not need to buy a bed if you have a crate, but some owners like to have a dog bed in the sitting room, for example, while the crate is kept in the kitchen or utility room. The most practical choice is a plastic, kidney-shaped bed. This is virtually indestructible, and, when it is lined with bedding, it makes a cosy bed for your pup.

FEEDING BOWLS

You will need two bowls – one for food and one for water. Plastic bowls are bright and colourful, but they tend to get chewed. Ceramic bowls look attractive, but they are breakable. Stainless steel bowls are easy to clean, and last a lifetime – so they are probably the best option.

COLLAR AND LEAD

Buy a soft, lightweight collar that you can adjust as your puppy grows. The lead should also be lightweight, but make sure it has a secure trigger fastening. Chain leads are best avoided as they are cumbersome, and can chafe your hands.

BRUSH AND COMB

A puppy's coat does not require much grooming, but your puppy needs to get used to the routine. Buy a soft-bristled baby brush, and you can use this until the adult coat comes through (see Chapter Five: Russell Basics).

Toys

Pet stores are full of fun toys for puppies, so you will be spoiled for choice. However, it is important to bear in mind that even small pups have sharp teeth, and they can reduce a toy to pieces in no time. This can be highly dangerous if the pup swallows a bit of plastic, or the squeaker from a toy. To avoid such problems, choose hard, rubber toys, or cotton tug-toys that are 100 per cent safe.

ID

Dogs are required by law to wear some form of identification which carries your contact details. You can arrange to get a disc engraved, or you may prefer to go for a permanent form of ID, such as a tattoo or a microchip implant. Ask your vet for information about these procedures.

FINDING A VET

If this is your first puppy, you will need to find a vet in your area. The breeder may be able to recommend a practice, or you may have doggy friends who can help. Before making your choice, visit the practice, and check out the following:

- Are the staff friendly and helpful?
- What provision is made for emergency cover?
- What facilities are available, e.g. X-ray, ultrasound, etc.?
- Do any of the vets have experience with Russells?

If you are happy with what you find, book an appointment for your pup to have a check-up a few days after he has arrived home.

PREPARING YOUR HOME

It is a good idea to decide in advance where your puppy is going to sleep. You will need to choose a place that is warm in the winter, cool

It is your job to keep temptation out of reach!

in the summer, and free from draughts. Most owners find the kitchen or utility room is the most suitable.

It is inevitable that your pup will investigate, and chew, everything that appears interesting or different. Try to see your home from a pup's perspective, and put anything that is valuable, or potentially hazardous, out of reach.

Check that the garden fencing is secure, and that the gate has a catch that works. Russells are hugely inquisitive, and will find the smallest gap to crawl through if they think there is something worth investigating. They are also great diggers, and will be happy to turn your garden into a minefield! To avoid this, you can provide a digging pit, which is rather like a children's sand-pit, and then train your pup to dig in his own special place. This is quite easy to do if you take the pup to the digging pit, and then let him see you bury a couple of treats. As your pup digs to find them, give the command "Dig". Repeat this on a number of occasions, and your pup will soon get the idea.

You will need to allocate an area in your garden for toilet training. If you take your pup to the same spot every time, it will help with his house-training (see pages 42-43). It also makes cleaning up easier if your dog only fouls one area.

COLLECTING YOUR PUPPY

The waiting is over, and at long last it is time to collect your Russell. Try to arrange to collect your pup as early in the day as possible, as this will give him plenty of time to settle into his new home before nightfall.

If possible, take a friend with you, so one person can hold the puppy, while the other concentrates on driving. You would also be advised to take a towel or some bedding for the pup to snuggle into, and some paper towels in case of accidents. If you have a long journey and the weather is warm, you should take a bowl and some drinking water.

Arrange to collect your puppy early in the day so that he has time to settle into his new home.

PAPERWORK

The breeder will probably have a 'puppy kit' prepared for you. This should include:

- The puppy's pedigree.
- Forms for transfer of ownership, and Kennel Club registration.
- Details of worming treatment to date.
- A diet sheet, outlining the schedule for feeding as your puppy matures.
- A sample of food – to keep changes to a minimum when your puppy is settling into his new home.
- Contact details for after-sales advice, if required.

THE JOURNEY HOME

If you have someone to hold your puppy, you will probably find that he will make a token protest and then settle down to sleep. Do not worry if he is a little car-sick; this is unlikely to be a long-term problem.

If you have to travel alone, the pup should be confined to a crate or a puppy carrier. He will certainly let you know he is there – but he will come to no harm if he is in secure accommodation.

Unless you have a long journey, it is better not to stop. If you do need to break the journey, remember that your pup is not vaccinated and must not be allowed on the ground.

Welcome Home!

There is always tremendous excitement when a puppy arrives in his new home, but it is important to try to keep things as calm as possible. The pup has been taken away from everything that is familiar, and he no longer has his brothers and sisters to rally round and give him confidence. For the first time, he is facing life on his own.

SETTLING IN

To begin with, give your pup a chance to explore the garden. He will almost certainly need to relieve himself, so give him lots of praise when he performs.

Give your pup the opportunity to investigate his new surroundings, and encourage him with lots of praise and reassurance. You can try calling your pup to you – while he feels vulnerable he will be quick to respond – and, in no time, he will have learnt his name.

When you go in the house, show your pup where you have located his crate or his bed, and tempt him to go in by offering a few treats. If he does as you ask, stroke him and give him lots of praise. Then give your pup a chance to explore his new home and meet his new 'pack'.

Start by giving your puppy a chance to explore the garden.

MEETING THE FAMILY

Although you will want to show off your new puppy to all your friends and neighbours, resist the temptation to do so for a couple of days. Give the pup a chance to meet the members of his new family before he takes on the rest of the world!

If you have young children, you must supervise all interactions. It is all too easy for a child to play too roughly, or for a puppy to get overexcited. To start with, sit the children on the floor, and provide them with the treats. They can then call the pup in turn, and give him a treat. This will certainly get relations off to a good start! Make sure the children are always sitting on the floor when they play with the pup. A wriggling pup could be dropped, and risk serious injury.

TEACHING RESPECT

It is essential that both the children and the puppy learn to respect each other. Obviously, this is required if your Russell is living in a family with children, but, even if this is not the case, you should make sure your pup has the opportunity to meet children, and to interact with them. You may well be in a situation, in the park for example, when you come across children, and your Russell must know how to behave.

Sometimes Russells have been accused of being short-tempered and snappy with children, but this reputation is entirely undeserved. If your pup is from sound stock, and has been well socialised with children, he will be affectionate and tolerant. The following exercise is useful for teaching good manners to all concerned.

- Give the child a treat to offer to the puppy. When the pup takes the treat, use a command such as "Be gentle".
- If the pup attempts to mouth or bite, intervene and say 'No'. Make sure the child only gives the treat when the pup is ready to take it gently. In this way, the pup will learn that he is not rewarded for being pushy. He only gets his treat when he is calm and gentle.
- You can then give the child a few treats to drop into the puppy's bowl while he is eating. The pup will be happy to get a bonus, and it will teach him not to become protective over his food bowl.

Toys can be a source of trouble, as games can quickly get out of hand. Again, it is essential to supervise all play sessions. You can also work at the following exercise.

- Give the child a treat, and start a game with a toy. Let the child and pup play for a couple of minutes.
- Tell the child to say "Give", and show the pup the treat. The puppy will drop the toy in favour of the treat, and he can be praised for a correct response.

Work on the above exercises over a period of time, and your puppy will learn that children must be respected. On the other side of the coin, the children must learn that the pup is not a toy that can be played with at will. Children must learn the following rules:

- The puppy must never be picked up (see above).

Both puppy and child must learn a sense of mutual respect.

- He must not be treated roughly, pulling his ears or his tail.
- He must not be disturbed when he is asleep.
- He must not be disturbed if he is eating (unless an adult is supervising a training exercise).

Once both children and puppy have learned a code of behaviour, you can look forward to enjoying family life, with your new puppy, to the full.

THE RESIDENT DOG

If you already have a dog at home, it is important to supervise the initial introduction. The best place for meeting is the garden, as this will give the dogs room to move. Make sure there are no toys or chews around, as these can quickly become a source of conflict.

Start off by letting your adult dog sniff the puppy. In most cases, the pup will be subservient, and may even roll over on to his back to show he is no threat.

A bolder pup may jump up at the adult, or he may even try to instigate a game. If the adult has a playful nature, he may respond to these overtures, but he may well give a warning growl, telling the pup to 'back off'.

Unless you are seriously concerned, do not interfere. It is much better to allow two dogs to sort out their own relationship. If you become over-protective of the pup, the adult is bound to feel that his nose has been put out of joint, and will resent the newcomer. Supervise interactions for a couple of days until you are confident that the pup has been fully accepted.

It is also important to spend some quality time with your adult dog playing with him, or running through some exercises. You can do this when you take him out for walks, as the pup will still be too young to take part in this activity. The adult will enjoy feeling special, and will realise that his role in the family has not been undermined.

FELINE FRIENDS

Dogs and cats are considered to be natural enemies, and most terriers feel they have a personal vendetta against the entire feline population. The terrier's hunting instinct is brought to the fore when a cat is in full flight – and the results can be disastrous.

If you have a cat, it is imperative to work at this relationship from the moment your Russell arrives home. He has to learn that cats must *never* be chased, under any circumstances.

- Start off with the puppy in a crate, and allow your cat to go up and investigate the new arrival. This will give her some confidence before formal introductions take place.
- Next, hold your puppy on your lap, and allow the cat into the same room. It will help if you can recruit a family member to hold the cat in fairly close proximity to the puppy.

If you supervise initial interactions, your puppy will learn that cats are not for chasing.

- Arm yourself with some treats, and every time the pup looks away from the cat, give him a treat. This will teach him that it is more rewarding to respond to you, rather than the cat.
- If the cat chooses to leave, allow her to do so, making sure the pup does not set off in hot pursuit.
- The next step is to allow the pup and cat to meet each other without being restrained. Obviously, this is a tense moment, but be ready with your treats so you can distract the pup from the cat.
- If the pup gets too boisterous, the cat will hiss, and may give him a quick swipe across the nose. Although you do not want your pup to be hurt, a swift lesson will work wonders.

Give this relationship time to establish itself. Do not leave your puppy and cat alone for the first few weeks, and do not allow them in the garden together until you know your Russell has learnt not to chase.

If you have on-going problems sorting out this relationship, you may need to seek the help of a professional dog trainer or behaviourist.

DIET AND FEEDING

The breeder will have given you a diet sheet, and you should follow this, at least to begin with, using the food that is recommended and feeding the quantity as directed. A puppy has so much to get used to when he is settling into his new home that it is important to keep changes to a minimum. The inevitable outcome of trying your pup on a new diet will be an upset stomach, which is obviously best avoided. If you do decide to change the type of food, do so gradually, adding a little of the new diet each day over four or five days until you make a complete transition.

There is a wide selection of dog food on the market, but, basically, there are three main types to choose from.

COMPLETE: This diet is easy to feed, and is carefully balanced to cater for all nutritional needs. You can get a diet specially formulated for puppies, and then move on to a maintenance diet when your Russell is full-grown. Do not attempt to supplement this diet with other types of food as it will upset the nutritional balance. Check the labelling for an analysis of the diet, and for the correct quantity to feed.

CANNED: There are so many different types of canned dog food available that you will need to look at the label for details of nutritional value. Canned food is generally fed with biscuit, which is good for your Russell's teeth.

Initially, changes to the diet should be kept to a minimum.

HOMEMADE: Some owners like to feed fresh meat with biscuit, or sometimes rice or pasta. This sounds fine in principle, but the danger is that you may not be feeding a correctly balanced diet for a puppy, and this could lead to problems. Unless you are prepared to go to a lot of trouble working out the nutritional value of what you are feeding, this is not a sensible option.

Obviously, the choice of diet is a matter of personal preference and convenience, as well as finding out what suits your Russell. Remember, your puppy's breeder will have considerable experience of rearing puppies, so their advice is well worth listening to.

MEALTIMES

You may find that your pup is reluctant to eat for the first couple of days. In most cases, this is simply because the puppy is preoccupied with getting used to his new surroundings, and he may also miss the rivalry of his littermates.

If your pup leaves his meal, wait for 10 minutes, and if he does not return to it, throw it away. Your pup will be hungry by the next mealtime and will probably eat with more relish. Remember to make fresh drinking water available at regular intervals. If your puppy is still refusing his food after a couple of days, consult your vet. Generally, a puppy of eight weeks will need four meals a day. This can be reduced to three meals when the pup is around 12 weeks of age. Try to space out these meals during the course of a day, and when possible keep to a regular routine. By six months, your Jack Russell will need two meals a day, fed in the morning and the evening.

CRATE TRAINING

Your Russell needs to get used to going into his crate, and staying in it for short periods. Make the crate as attractive as possible, lining it

Your puppy is more likely to settle in his crate if you give him some toys to play with.

with bedding, and putting in a toy or a chew. Encourage your pup to go into his crate, and stay with him, stroking him, and leaving the door open. You can then progress to shutting the door, but staying in the room for a few minutes. In most cases, you will find that your pup is so tired with the adventures of the day that he will settle down for a sleep.

Some pups take longer than others to accept the crate, but keep on trying, and only leave your pup for short periods. Never use the crate as a means of punishment; the aim is for your pup to regard the crate as his own doggy den, where he can rest undisturbed.

THE FIRST NIGHT

It is very hard for an eight-week-old puppy to settle on his own for the night, without the comfort of his littermates. Whatever policy you adopt, you will have to resign yourself to some vocal protests, but, in this situation, it pays to be firm.

- Give your puppy his last meal around 9pm, otherwise he will get hungry during the night.
- Have a last game with your pup, and then take him out to relieve himself.
- Tempt your puppy into his crate (or his dog bed) with a treat, and then close the door on him. You can leave him with a toy to play with.
- If your pup is to sleep in a dog bed in the kitchen or utility room, do a last-minute check to ensure there is nothing dangerous that he could chew, or places where he could get stuck.

Inevitably your puppy will cry, but if you go down to comfort him he will cry even harder next time, in the hope that this will bring you to him. If your puppy is in a crate, you can be certain that he can come to no harm, so the best plan is to put in some ear-plugs, and wait for morning!

It is inevitable that your pup will feel lost and bewildered when he is left alone at night for the first time.

If you do not make a big fuss, your pup will soon get used to the routine, and he will accept that the world does not fall apart when he is left on his own.

This is not only important so that you can get a good night's sleep, it also means that your pup will be happy to be left alone for short periods during the day, which is essential for his future wellbeing.

Puppies that do not learn to cope on their own become very anxious and insecure, and this can lead to behavioural problems in adulthood.

HOUSE-TRAINING

You can start work on this as soon as your Russell arrives home. Take your pup to the area you have allocated for toilet training, and, when he performs, give the command "Be clean" or "Busy".

Then reward your pup with lots of praise, and maybe have a game with him before going into the house.

Repeat this on every occasion you take your pup into the garden, and he will soon understand what is required.

It is important to take your pup out at regular intervals during the day. These include:

- After every meal
- When your puppy wakes up
- After a play session
- Every two hours.

If you work hard at house-training, your puppy will soon understand what is required.

This may sound like a punishing schedule, but the harder you work in the early stages, the quicker your puppy will learn to be clean. The key is to be vigilant, and if you see your puppy circling or sniffing when he is in the house, the chances are that he needs to go out. In this way, you will keep accidents to a minimum, and your puppy will realise that his toilet area is in the garden.

If your puppy has an accident in the house, do not shout at him. It is likely to be your fault for not seeing that he needed to go out. If you catch him 'red-handed', take him outside immediately, and wait until he performs. Then give him lots of praise.

It may take a while for your puppy to be clean at night as, to begin with, he is simply not mature enough to go through the night. However, if you use a crate, this process will be a lot quicker, as a dog hates to foul his sleeping quarters.

Do not make the mistake of believing you have cracked house-training, and waiting for your pup to ask to go outside. You will need to do the thinking for him for a few months until he is totally reliable.

Starting Right

Owning a well-behaved, adaptable dog, who is a pleasure to be with, is not a matter of luck. Good owners equal good dogs – and the more effort you put into training and socialising your Russell, the better he will turn out.

Do not look on training as a chore, otherwise it will become just that. It is fun time, when you can interact with your dog and build up a closer relationship.

GOLDEN RULES

A dog needs to know where he stands in terms of his place in the family, and as regards general behaviour. You cannot expect your Russell to play by the rules if no-one has told him what they are. For this reason, it is important to establish a sense of leadership from the start, so that your pup knows where the authority is coming from. Dogs are pack animals, and although they have been domesticated for thousands of years, every dog instinctively understands a social hierarchy. Every pack must have a leader, and all other members must sort out their relative rankings. When your Russell comes into your family, he is looking to see how he fits into his new pack. It is important that you are ready to provide an answer, which you will demonstrate in the way you behave towards your pup.

- Give your pup a clear lead, praising desirable behaviour, and being firm when he misbehaves.
- Make sure that all members of the family follow the same policy so that the pup learns to respect all members of his pack, regardless of their size or age.
- Be 100 per cent consistent when you are dealing with your pup. This means always giving the same commands for behaviour you want, and being firm when your pup does something inappropriate.

Give your pup a sense of leadership so that he learns his place in the family 'pack'.

There are times when a dog is deliberately disobedient, but there are many more times when he is completely confused because of his owner's inconsistent attitude. For example, a pup is encouraged to jump up to say hello, until the time he does it with muddy paws – and then he gets a good telling-off. It is hardly surprising that the puppy becomes puzzled, and fails to respect his leader. In time, this dog may decide to challenge his own subservient status, and the result is a complete breakdown of the human-canine relationship.

The Russell is a quick-witted, intelligent dog, so make sure you start as you mean to go on. Sort out the house rules, e.g. whether your pup is allowed to go on the furniture, sleep on the bed, etc., and make sure you always give the same message. Most dogs are content to accept authority, and will quickly learn desirable behaviour.

REWARD-BASED TRAINING

When you start training, you must tune into the Russell's mind. We like to think that all dogs are eager to please, and that may be true of some breeds. However, the Russell is pretty keen on pleasing himself. Why should he come when he is called when he has just discovered an interesting scent?

You need to find a way of changing the terrier mind-set, so that your Russell *wants* to do as you ask. The best way of doing this is to find out what your pup likes best. It could be a ball, or a squeaky toy that he has taken a fancy to, or he may be ruled by his stomach so that treats are the answer. Whatever it is, make sure you give it as a reward when you are training. Your pup will learn that if he does as you ask, he gets double points – you are pleased with him and praise him, plus he gets a game with his toy or a mouthwatering treat.

CLICKER TRAINING

This is a method of training that is proving hugely successful, and it suits the Russell in particular. It is based on the concept of positive reinforcement, using the conditioned response of the clicker.

The clicker is a small box, with a 'click' mechanism which you operate with your thumb. To begin with, you teach your pup to associate the click with getting a treat. This builds up a conditioned response, so that the pup knows that every time he hears a click, a reward will follow.

The next step is to use the clicker to mark appropriate behaviour. If your pup does something you want him to do, such as sitting, give a click, and this acts as a 'yes' marker, telling the pup he has offered the correct behaviour and a treat will follow.

A puppy needs to be motivated to do as you ask.

As training progresses, you can introduce cues or commands so that your pup gives the correct behaviour when you ask for it. The applications of clicker training are far-reaching; it can be used in all aspects of training, from Competitive Obedience and Agility to just teaching your pup to perform a trick. The Russell, who is ever-alert and ready for something new to interest him, is an ideal pupil.

There are now many clubs that specialise in clicker training, so this may be well worth investigating (see page 47).

BASIC EXERCISES

All puppies need to be taught elementary obedience, regardless of your long-term ambitions. This will give your Russell a grounding in good manners, and once you have mastered the basics, you can progress to a more advanced level if you wish. Remember that a puppy has a short concentration span, and it is much better to train little and often, rather than attempting a lengthy session.

The following exercises can be taught with or without a clicker. The most important point is that training is reward-based, using either a toy or a treat depending on your Russell's preference. For the sake of clarity, treats are used when outlining the following exercises.

SIT

This is the simplest exercise to teach, so it makes a good starting point.

- Get a treat and hold it just above your puppy's head.
- As your pup looks up and tries to reach the treat, he will start to lower his rear end.
- He will naturally go into the Sit, and then you can click and reward. Work on this a few times, so that your pup understands that the Sit is the behaviour you want. Click and reward for every correct response.
- When your pup is sitting reliably, you can introduce the verbal command "Sit" to coincide with the action. Your pup will be quick to make the association, and will soon learn to "Sit" on cue.

If you hold a treat above your puppy's head, he will naturally go into the Sit.

Use a treat to lure your
puppy into the Down.

DOWN

This is a natural progression of the Sit exercise. Do not start to teach it until you are confident that your pup has mastered the Sit.

- Start with your pup in the Sit, and show him that you have a treat in your closed hand.
- Use your hand to lure your puppy towards the ground. To begin with, the front end will go down. At this stage, you can click and reward to encourage your pup to repeat the behaviour.
- Eventually the pup will follow the treat all the way to the ground, and will go into the Down. Click and reward.
- As with the Sit, you can introduce the verbal command once the behaviour has become established.

STAY

When your pup is happy with the Sit and the Down commands, you can work at extending the length of time he stays in position. You can do this when your pup is in either the Sit or the Down; the key is to build up the Stay exercise in easy stages.

- Start with your pup in the Sit (or Down), but this time wait a few moments before you click and reward.
- Repeat the exercise, this time stepping a pace away from your pup. You can help your pup to understand what is required by giving a hand signal, (palm held upright towards him). Step back to your pup's side, and then click and reward.
- The duration of this exercise can be built up gradually. You can also introduce variations, such as walking in a circle around your pup,

or stepping over him, so that he becomes really secure in the Stay.

- The verbal command can be introduced when your pup has fully understood the exercise.

COME

Make sure you keep this exercise completely separate from the Stay, or you will end up with a very confused puppy!

In fact, teaching your pup to come is a lesson to start on day one. Puppies have a natural instinct to follow, and, in the first few days after arriving home, your puppy will follow you everywhere. You can make use of this by using your pup's name, and giving the command "Come", and your pup will be quick to respond. Carry your clicker in your pocket, and then you can click and reward when your pup responds. Always give lots of praise, as you want to build up a really

The Stay should be worked on in easy stages.

strong response to this command before you venture into the outside world when your pup is fully inoculated (see pages 97-101).

A Russell has a will of his own, and this is most particularly apparent when he gets on the trail of an interesting scent. Some Russell owners do not trust their dogs off the lead in an open environment, but there are ways of working on the Come exercise so that your Russell becomes more reliable.

- Always reward your pup for coming to you. You can give him a treat, or have a game with a favourite toy. Your Russell needs to learn that coming to you means fun.

It is essential to build up a really strong response to the "Come" command.

- You can reinforce the "Come" command by using it at mealtimes, or when you are going out in the car, so that your Russell associates the command with the things he likes most.
- When you try a recall off-lead in the park, tie a training line (a length of rope measuring 9-12 ft), to your puppy's collar. Recruit an assistant, and ask them to hold your pup by the collar. Walk a short distance away, and call your puppy. The moment you call, the assistant should release the puppy – and you should be ready to click and reward as your pup comes in to you. The training line is not used to reel the puppy in, but it can be used, if necessary, to stop your puppy running away. It is much better to teach your pup if he does not have the opportunity to misbehave.
- When your pup is coming reliably, you can discard the training line. With luck, your pup will show the same enthusiastic response, as he knows this brings a reward. However, if your pup gets distracted, or is slow coming to you, do not punish him when he finally reaches you – no matter how long he takes. Your pup will not connect his poor response with the punishment; he will think he is being told off for returning to you.

- When you are on a walk, call your Russell to you at intervals, and reward him with a treat or a game, before he is allowed to go free again. This will teach him that coming to you is a fun part of the outing – it does not signify the end of the walk and being put back on the lead.

LEAD-TRAINING

Again, this is something you can work at while you are waiting for your pup to complete his inoculations. This will mean that your Russell will be walking happily on a lead by the time you are ready to go out and about.

PUTTING ON THE COLLAR

Start by putting on the collar for a few moments. You can click and reward your pup as soon as the collar is fastened, or you can distract his attention by playing a game with him. Most puppies scratch the collar a bit to begin with, but they soon get used to it. It may help if you feed your puppy a meal while he is wearing his collar – that will certainly keep his mind occupied!

Accustom your pup to wearing his collar for short sessions, until he has learnt to ignore it.

ATTACHING THE LEAD

Try attaching the lead in the house to begin with, making sure your pup does not get tangled up on pieces of furniture.

- Allow your pup to move around, with the lead trailing, making sure he is closely supervised.
- Pick up the lead and follow your pup wherever he wants to go.
- Next, encourage your pup to walk with you. Some pups respond immediately. If this happens, you can click and reward, and make a big fuss of your pup, before moving on again.

Be ready to reward your pup when he starts to walk with you on the lead.

- If your pup puts on the brakes, do not try to force him to walk with you – a Russell can be very stubborn! Instead, offer him a treat, or show him a toy, and encourage him to come to you. Click and reward him for any movement towards you. As soon as you have some signs of success, make a big fuss of your pup, and end the training session. It is important not to overtax a young puppy, particularly if he is finding a lesson difficult.

- Keep repeating the above exercise, several times a day, until your pup is happy to walk with you. Make sure that your pup understands that walking next to you on a loose lead is the best place to be, by stopping and rewarding him when he is in the correct position.

- If your pup tries to surge ahead, do not attempt to pull him back into position. Stop and call your pup to you. As soon as he moves towards you, click to mark a correct response. When he is back by your side, click and reward before moving off.

Obviously, it takes a while before your pup learns to walk on a loose lead in all situations. When you go on your first outings, you will almost certainly find that your pup regresses in his training as he tries to take in all the new sights and sounds. Be patient, and be ready to encourage and reward him at every opportunity. In time, your pup will learn to trust you, and will enjoy working with you as a team.

RETRIEVE

This is not such an important exercise to teach in terms of basic obedience, but your Russell will enjoy learning a new game, and it provides a means of easy exercise. Teach the retrieve in easy stages, working on each stage before moving on to the next.

- Find a favourite toy, and get your dog really excited about it: play a game of tug, hide it behind your back, and throw it a short distance. When your Russell shows any interest in the toy, click and reward. Remember, this is a game, so make it fun, giving lots of praise and encouragement.
- The next step is for your Russell to hold the toy and to give it back to you on command. Have a game with the toy, and, when your Russell holds the toy, click and reward. When he has learnt to take the toy from you, you can introduce the command "Hold".
- Now you want your dog to hold his toy, and then release it on command. Practise taking the toy from your Russell, and click and reward when he gives it up without a struggle. When he has understood what is required, introduce the command "Give".
- By now, your Russell should be really focused on his toy, so introducing "Fetch" should be fairly straightforward. Throw the toy a short distance, and click as soon as your Russell runs out towards the toy. Click again for picking up the toy. As your Russell gets the idea of what he is meant to do, you will not have to click for every stage.
- At this point, some dogs think it is a great idea to run off with the toy rather than bringing it back. Generally, a clicker-trained dog is quick to change his behaviour if you stop clicking – and no treats are forthcoming. With a little encouragement, your Russell will

This may seem a bit of a formal exercise just for getting your Russell out of the car. But it serves two purposes: it teaches your dog good manners, and it avoids the risk of a serious accident which could happen if your Russell was allowed to leap out without proper supervision.

TRAINING CLASSES

Once your Russell is fully vaccinated, you can join a training club. This will give you the opportunity to get advice from experienced handlers, and your puppy will learn to work alongside other dogs.

Before taking your pup along, attend a session so that you can watch the instructors at work. It is important to ensure that reward-based training methods are used, and that the classes are well organised. A young puppy will benefit from interacting with other dogs, but should be protected from individuals that have a tendency to bully.

If you plan to compete in one of the canine sports (see Chapter Six: Having Fun with your Russell), you will need to master basic obedience before joining a club that specialises in the activity of your choice.

ALL-ROUND EDUCATION

Training is a vital part of your Russell's upbringing, but this must go hand in hand with a programme of socialisation. You cannot expect your pup to develop into a well-balanced, adaptable adult unless you teach him the ways of the world. Any self-respecting terrier would dedicate himself to chasing cats, stealing food, and disappearing down the nearest hole – unless he was taught that this constituted undesirable behaviour.

As previously discussed, a dog is prepared to accept the authority of his leader, and he will learn to live by the rules. Your task is to expose your pup to as many different situations as possible so that you can teach appropriate behaviour.

A puppy that is exposed to a variety of different experiences will mature into a well-balanced, adaptable adult.

This process should start in the breeder's home. The puppies should be handled as much as possible, and be accustomed to the sights and sounds of a busy household. When your pup arrives home, you must continue with this, supervising his interactions with the family and any resident pets (see pages 36-38), and making sure that he gets used to all the different machines in the house (e.g. the washing machine and the vacuum cleaner). He needs to get used to being handled all over, and you should give a regular groom with a soft-bristled brush so that he gets used to the routine.

Once your pup has had a chance to settle in, you can invite visitors to meet the new arrival. This will broaden his knowledge of the human race, and you can teach him the right way to behave, i.e. not barking or jumping up, but sitting to be stroked in a civilised manner.

Many veterinary practices hold puppy socialisation parties, and this provides an excellent opportunity for your puppy to meet other people, and to interact with puppies of a similar age. Generally,

The Russell is often known as the 'stable terrier', and, if correctly socialised, he will live happily alongside horses.

puppies are allowed to attend after they have had their first inoculation.

When your pup is ready to go out into the outside world, you can step up his programme of socialisation. Here are a few suggestions as to what you can do.

- Go to a shopping centre and sit on a bench with your puppy. This will allow him to watch everything that is going on, while being reassured by your presence. Few people can resist a puppy, so he will also meets lots of different people.

- Go to a park and let your puppy watch children playing in the recreation area. Your pup will hear the shouts and screams of children at play, and will learn that this is nothing to be concerned about.

- As your pup gets more confident, go to areas of heavy traffic, and try to pass by some roadworks. If your puppy is concerned by the noise, be ready to give encouragement. You can also distract his attention by giving him a treat.

- Go to a railway station, or a bus station, so your pup gets used to the noise and the crowds.
- Make sure your Russell meets some livestock, such as sheep, cattle, or poultry. Obviously, your pup will be on a lead, and you can be quick to correct any efforts to pull towards the animals. Make sure you have lots of treats so that you can reward your pup when he looks away from the animals and focuses his attention on you.

If your pup shows signs of concern when you are socialising him, do not make the mistake of making a big fuss – otherwise he will think that there really is something to worry about. Adopt a calm and relaxed manner, and gently reassure your pup, possibly distracting his attention with a treat. Do not force him to go up to whatever is frightening him; just show him that there is nothing to worry about, and allow him to proceed at his own pace. In most cases, initial hesitation is soon overcome.

Use every opportunity to take your puppy out and about for the first 12 months of his life. He will benefit enormously from receiving a broad education, and you will also improve your relationship with him by spending time together.

When your Russell has grown up, do not leave him at home thinking he has learnt everything that is required. Although the first 12 months are the most significant, your dog will continue to learn throughout his life – and he does not want to miss the chance of a trip out!

COPING WITH ADOLESCENCE

Assuming you have worked hard at training and socialising your Russell, he should be well on the way to becoming an ideal companion by the time he is around six months of age. Then, all of a sudden, adolescence strikes, and you seem to be moving one step forward – and several steps back.

The Russell has a mind of his own, and he can become intent on pleasing himself.

The time at which a dog becomes adolescent varies between individuals, but the signs are easy to spot. A male will start to lift his leg to mark his territory, and may well become more assertive in his dealings with other dogs – and with people. A female may become moody and withdrawn as she approaches her first season; she may also 'forget' basic training as she becomes more interested in pleasing herself.

As your Russell becomes sexually mature, it is inevitable that he/she will look at the world through different eyes. Like a human teenager, an adolescent dog will start to question established authority, and will cease to be the co-operative individual you once cherished.

Do not despair, your wonderful Russell is not lost forever! In fact, he may be his normal self for most of the time, and just show occasional changes in character. However, you should not ignore this stage, simply looking forward to the time when the hormones have settled down. You must try to understand what is going on in your Russell's mind, and be ready to reinforce training when it breaks down.

REDUCING DOMINANCE

There are many different ways a dog may express adolescent behaviour:
- He could forget his manners and start lying on the sofa.
- He might start jumping up and barking at visitors.
- He may start becoming possessive about his toys or his food.
- He may turn a 'deaf' ear when you call him back at the end of a walk.

Obviously, each type of behaviour should be dealt with separately, making it clear that it is inappropriate, and reinforcing a correct response with praise and treats. However, there is a common cause of the problems and it needs to be tackled.

Basically, your Russell is attempting to assert his own will and usurp your leadership. In the wild, a pack leader would face regular challenges from adolescent pretenders, and he would be quick to re-establish his own authority. In a domestic situation, dealing with your Russell, you must do exactly the same. You can reinforce your position as leader in the following ways.

- Always feed your family before giving your Russell his meal.
- Every time you go through a door, command your dog to "Wait", so that you go through first.
- When you travel in the car, make sure your dog does not get out of the car until you allow him to.
- When your dog is feeding, take his bowl away for a few moments, and then let him have it back again.

- Do not let your Russell sleep on the bed or on the furniture.
- When you play with your dog, make sure you end up with the toy.
- Set aside a session for training every day so that you have the opportunity to reward your Russell for desirable behaviour.

These measures may seem insignificant in themselves, but together they build up a picture of control and authority. You are also giving your Russell the chance to behave correctly, so you can give him a treat or have a game with him. This gives your Russell the incentive to co-operate; if he does as you ask, he gets what he wants.

Neutering is an option that is worth considering.

NEUTERING

If you do not plan to breed with your Russell, you may wish to consider the option of neutering. Veterinary practices have different policies as to when is the best time to neuter. Generally, a bitch is spayed after she has had her first season, and midway before the next season is due. A male is usually castrated at around nine months, when he is sexually mature. The advantages are numerous for both males and females:

- There is no seasonal cycle to cope with.
- In males, the risk of developing prostate disorders or testicular cancer is reduced.
- In females, the risk of mammary tumours is reduced, and there is no danger of developing pyometra – a life-threatening condition where the womb fills with pus.
- It may help with behavioural problems in males.

The possible downside is that neutered dogs have a tendency to put on weight, but this can easily be prevented by controlling the diet.

Obviously, this is a big decision to make, so you would be wise to ask your vet for advice.

Routine Care

The Russell is a fit little dog, and, given the right care, he will live a long life and suffer few health problems. However, the quality of his life is in your hands – so you must work hard at providing for all his needs.

KNOW YOUR DOG

Prevention is better than cure, and this is 100 per cent the case when you are looking after a dog. Every breed is different, and all dogs are individuals, so you need to know what is right for your own dog. You will know what food suits him, how much exercise he needs, and whether he is feeling in tip-top health.

You can add to this knowledge by examining your Russell on a regular basis. The best time to do this is when you are grooming. Use the opportunity to check for the following:

- Any unusual lumps or bumps.
- Signs of flea infestation (see pages 101-102).
- Signs of hair loss or soreness.
- The eyes should be bright and sparkling with no discharge or

inflammation.
- The nose should be free from discharge and there should be no evidence of cracks or crustiness.
- Look into the ears to ensure they are clean and fresh-smelling.
- Check the teeth for accumulation of tartar or sore gums.
- Pick up each foot in turn, and check the pads for cuts or cracks.

Remember, the earlier you detect a problem, the quicker it can be treated, and the outcome is far more likely to be successful.

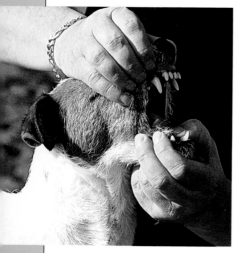

The teeth must be kept clean in order to avoid dental decay and gum disease.

DENTAL CARE

When your Russell puppy first arrives home, he will have his milk teeth, which are as sharp as needles. By the time he is around four months of age, these will drop out to be replaced by his adult teeth. Teething is a difficult time for most puppies. The gums are often sore, and the pup has a great desire to chew while the new teeth are erupting. Make sure you provide suitable toys and chews during this period – and keep your valuables well out of reach!

If you are feeding a complete diet, you will probably find that your Russell's teeth need regular cleaning, as he will not have the opportunity to keep them clean by chewing and gnawing. You can buy a long-handled toothbrush, or a finger brush, and some meaty toothpaste that is made specially for dogs.

Accustom your pup to having his teeth cleaned from an early age, and he will learn to accept the procedure. If he shows initial reluctance, work up to the job in easy stages, first opening his mouth, then brushing for a second, and then for a little longer, rewarding him with a treat at each stage. Your pup will soon get the idea that teeth-cleaning is a worthwhile occupation.

NAILS

If you exercise your Russell on hard surfaces, or do a lot of road walking, you may find that his nails wear down naturally. If they grow too long, they will need to be trimmed. This can be done using a nail file, or guillotine-type nail-clippers. It is important to trim only the tips of the nails or you will cut into the quick, which will bleed profusely.

If you have not trimmed nails before, ask your vet to show you what to do.

The Russell will learn to accept routine nail-trimming.

COAT CARE

The Russell is a relatively low-maintenance breed in terms of routine grooming. The puppy coat does not need much attention, but it is important that you groom at least once a week, so that your pup gets accustomed to all-over handling.

When the adult coat comes through, it will feel harsh to the touch, regardless of whether your Russell is smooth-coated, broken- or rough-coated. The best brush to use is a slicker brush, which is fine and wire-toothed. Plan your grooming session methodically, starting at the front of the dog, working your way down through the body and finishing with the hindquarters. Make sure you brush both the harsh topcoat and the thick undercoat. If you come across any mats or tangles, these can be teased out using a narrow-toothed comb.

Make sure you groom your Russell at least once a week, and this should be increased to a daily session when the coat is shedding.

Above: A slicker brush is used to work through the coat.

Left: A narrow-toothed comb can be used for teasing out tangles, or loosening the hair when the coat is shedding.

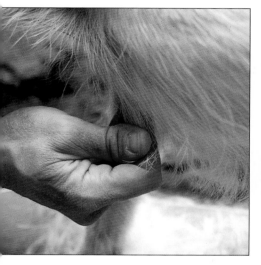

The hair can be plucked out using finger and thumb.

A stripping knife can be used to take out the loose coat.

STRIPPING

Rough- or broken-coated Russells will need to have their coat stripped. This is done when the coat is shedding, usually in the spring, but the coat will probably need further attention on at least one other occasion in the year.

The traditional method of stripping is using finger and thumb and plucking out the dead hair. This is completely painless for the dog, as long as it coincides with when the coat is shedding. A stripping knife can also be used to take out the dead hair. Russells that are exhibited in the show ring are always hand-stripped, as this gives the most natural effect, which is correct for the breed's working heritage.

The pet owner can cut down on the labour by employing the services of a professional groomer who will clip the coat. If you go for this option, make sure you go to a groomer that is used to working with Russells. Even if you are not showing your Russell, you still want him to look like a typical specimen of the breed.

BATHING

A white dog that likes going down holes is not a great combination, and it is inevitable that your Russell will get muddy and dirty. However, a bath should be the last resort, not the first. When the coat is dry, a good brush will get rid of most of the dirt, and this will be far better for the coat. If you bath your Russell too frequently, the coat will become soft rather than being the correct harsh, weatherproof jacket. For this reason, it is best to reserve bathtimes for the occasions when your Russell has rolled in something foul – and then you really have no choice!

- The Russell is small enough to be bathed in a sink, or you can use a shower cubicle. Place a rubber mat for your dog to stand on, as this will stop him slipping.
- Make sure the water is lukewarm, and soak the coat thoroughly.
- Apply the shampoo (always use a shampoo that is made specially for dogs), and work into a rich lather. Be careful to keep soap away from the head.
- Rinse the coat, making sure you get rid of all traces of shampoo.
- Before you allow your Russell to leave the bathing area, soak up the excess moisture from his coat with a towel.
- After your Russell has had a good shake, the coat can be towel-dried, or you can use a hair-dryer, making sure it is on a moderate setting.

Your Russell may not enjoy bathtimes, but, if you give him lots of praise and encouragement, he will learn to tolerate them. It is a good idea to bath your Russell while he is still a youngster, so that he gets used to the routine.

FEEDING REGIME

By now, you will have found the diet that best suits your Russell, and he should look forward to his meals as the highspots of his day. When your Russell is fully grown, you can cut down to one meal a day, but most owners prefer to split the rations into two meals, and feed in the morning and in the evening. This gives the stomach less to cope with at a time, and most dogs enjoy two big moments in the day!

Do not make the mistake of overfeeding your Russell. The breed is small in size, and has a very efficient metabolism, doing well on relatively small quantities. The greatest danger to health is obesity, and, unfortunately, there are far too many Russells that suffer from this problem. The following tips should help your Russell to stay lean and fit:

The Russell should be kept in lean, athletic condition.

- Always feed the same quantity, ensuring that your Russell eats all his food in one session.
- Do not leave discarded food out in case your Russell wants some more later.
- Never feed your Russell between meals, or when you are eating.
- If you are using treats for training, deduct the food from his daily ration.

Harden your heart, and resist those appealing brown eyes. A lean dog is a healthy dog.

BONES AND CHEWS

Gnawing on a bone is a great way of keeping teeth clean and gums healthy, and it also provides enjoyable occupation for your Russell. However, you must be careful what you give. Never allow your dog to have poultry bones, as these splinter and can cause considerable damage. Marrow-bones are ideal, and most dogs enjoy the sterilised bones which are filled with a meaty paste.

Chews are fine, but some dogs tend to chew off small pieces, which could cause problems. It is therefore safer to choose the hard, nylon type, which can only be chewed down gradually over a period of time.

Dogs can become possessive over bones, so make sure your Russell accepts that you are in charge of his bone, and he will give it up without complaint.

EXERCISE

The Russell was bred to run with the hunt, following horses on day-long excursions over rough terrain. Despite his small size, the Russell is a remarkably active dog with tremendous powers of endurance – you will tire long before he does!

There is no need to set a gruelling schedule of exercise while your

Russell is growing. A small dog is not so vulnerable to bone and joint disorders as the bigger breeds, but exercise should be limited for the first eight months or so. To begin with, a puppy will get as much exercise as he needs playing in the garden. When he has completed his vaccination course, you can introduce lead-walking, but you will find that a 10- to 15-minute session is more than sufficient.

If you have a safe place to free-run your Russell, this a great bonus. But you must ensure he is reliable on the recall before letting him off the lead. Again, do not allow your Russell to overexercise. A 15-minute run will allow him to let off steam without becoming exhausted.

Some Russell owners favour using an extending lead, which gives the dog a chance to explore, but you still remain in control. Practise using the extending lead in the garden so that you get used to it before trying it in a more challenging environment. For safety's sake, do not use the extending lead when you are walking alongside traffic.

SWIMMING

Terriers are not natural swimmers like the retrieving breeds, but some show a real liking for it. You will probably find that, if your Russell enjoys retrieving, he will be happy to take the plunge to fetch his toy.

Make sure the water you choose is safe, with no strong currents. It is also important that you find an easy place for your Russell to get in and out of the water.

PLAYING GAMES

Exercise does not have to take the form of a route march. Your Russell will expend lots of energy playing games with you; he will also benefit from the mental stimulation that this type of activity provides.

Be inventive, and think up some fun games you can play at home. These can range from a simple tug-of-war or retrieve, to a more complex game of hide-and-seek, using a trail of treats.

The Russell is an energetic dog who loves the opportunity to run.

Playing games will exercise your Russell's mind as well as his body.

Watch out for rabbit holes – few Russells can resist them!

TAKING THE PLUNGE!

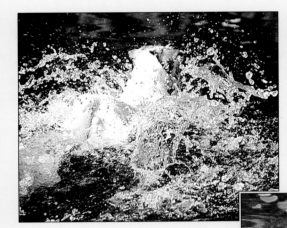

Some Russells love swimming, and this provides an excellent form of exercise. Make sure the place you choose is 100 per cent safe.

If you have a dog that thrives on being given things to do, you should consider getting involved in one of the specialist canine activities (see Chapter Six: Having Fun with your Russell).

THE VETERAN RUSSELL

Fortunately, Russells are a long-lived breed, and your dog should stay fit and active until he reaches double figures. Some individuals may carry on for another couple of years without showing any signs of slowing up; others may start to show their age earlier.

As a responsible owner, you need to be sensitive to the changing needs of your dog. A Russell is so determined that he may try to keep up with the pace, even when it is against his interests. Work out how much exercise your Russell needs, and turn for home when your dog is still bright and enthusiastic. If your dog has got wet, he will appreciate being dried when you return home, as some dogs tend to get a bit stiff in old age.

Your Russell will not need so much food as he gets older, so you must monitor his diet to ensure that he does not become overweight. Many of the food manufacturers provide a diet especially for veterans, and this may suit your dog in his later years.

The older Russell deserves special consideratio

SAYING GOODBYE

With luck, your Russell will live to around 14 years of age; many Russells do even better than this. However, a time will inevitably come when the quality of life starts to deteriorate. Medical science has advanced dramatically, and many more conditions can be successfully treated. But eventually, the body begins to pack up, and there is little enjoyment left in life.

It is vital to recognise these signs, and then to make the selfless decision of having your dog put to sleep. Of course, you want to keep your beloved Russell alive for as long as possible, but you must put his interests first. When the time comes, you must allow your dog to end his days with dignity.

It is never easy to get over the loss of a dog that has been your companion for more than a decade. But, eventually, you will be able to look back and recall all the happy times you spent together. Do not feel you are betraying your dog's memory by getting a puppy when you feel ready – it is the greatest compliment you can pay him.

Having Fun With Your Russell

The Russell is a highly intelligent and versatile dog, enjoying nothing more than a good challenge to stimulate body and mind. Without suitable occupation, he can become bored, which may lead to destructive behaviour. However, one of the joys of owning a Russell is the range of activities open to the breed.

CANINE GOOD CITIZEN

One of the best places to start is the Canine Good Citizen (CGC) Scheme, which is run in the UK and the US. The scheme was introduced to encourage responsible dog ownership; dogs with a CGC certificate carry proof of their good manners both at home and in the wider community.

To obtain a CGC certificate, dogs must pass a series of 'Good Citizen' tests, which involve basic obedience exercises and routine handling (such as grooming), acceptance of people and other dogs, and reacting calmly to crowded places and other distractions.

Many training clubs run the scheme; your national Kennel Club will be able to give you information on participating clubs in your area.

*The sweet,
gentle nature of
the Russell
comes to the fore
in therapy work.*

THERAPY DOGS

In recent years, there has been a big growth in the use of animals in therapy. Therapy dogs are now a relatively common sight in nursing homes and hospitals, and the important benefits they bring to the mental and physical health of patients is now starting to be recognised.

Many patients and elderly residents are deprived of their own pets, and the chance to stroke a dog and chat to the dog's owner brings great comfort. Therapy dogs are also being used in schools, helping pupils to learn how to react to animals, as well as finding out about the responsibilities of dog ownership.

To become a therapy dog, your Russell will need to be reliable, calm and friendly, well trained and responsive. Therapy work is very rewarding for the owner, and if your dog's temperament is suited to the task, he should enjoy the experience enormously – all those people making a fuss of him!

Agility is a fun sport for both dog and owner.

COMPETITION OBEDIENCE

By the time your Russell reaches adulthood, he should already be well trained in basic obedience. You may find that you want to develop this further, possibly moving on to competition level. Russells, with their natural intelligence, benefit enormously from further training.

One of the most popular types of advanced training is Competition Obedience. This involves precision heelwork, recalls, retrieves, stays, send-aways and scent discrimination. In the US, there is also an Agility section.

If you are interested in training for Competition Obedience, you will need to find a club that specialises in this discipline.

AGILITY

This is one of the most enjoyable forms of advanced training, and Russells love it. An Agility course is basically an obstacle course, which the dog must negotiate in as short a time as possible. The obstacles include tunnels, hurdles and weaving poles, as well as 'contact' obstacles – where the dog must get on and off the obstacle in a marked area – such as an A-frame, a see-saw (teeter), and a dog walk. For small breeds competing in Agility (which includes Russells), the height of the hurdles is lowered.

Before you start planning an Agility career for your Russell, you must work hard at basic obedience training. Your Russell needs to be 100 per cent reliable on the recall in order to work effectively off-lead when he is tackling an Agility course.

When you join an Agility club, the club's instructor will teach you and your Russell how to tackle the course. However, training should not be started until your dog is fully mature. The UK's Kennel Club prohibits dogs less than 18 months from competing, while, in the US, the AKC has an age barrier of one year. Physical fitness applies to the owner as well – remember that you will need to be pretty fit to keep up with your Russell as he runs the course at speed!

Fast and accurate, the Russell is a great Flyball competitor.

FLYBALL

Flyball is a canine relay race over hurdles. Two teams compete against each other, and the winner is the team to finish in the fastest time. Each dog must clear a set of hurdles to reach a Flyball box at the other end of the track. At the box, the dog triggers a device to release a ball. The dog catches the ball in his mouth, and then clears the hurdles back to the starting line. If a dog drops the ball, fails to clear a hurdle, or starts before his predecessor has crossed the finish line, he will have to run the course again.

Flyball is great fun for the dog, and it has also proved to be an exciting spectator sport. Russells are proving themselves to be adept competitors – their exuberant level of energy and enthusiasm is ideally suited to the sport.

The working ability of the Russell can be tested in Earth Dog events.

EARTH DOG COMPETITIONS

Earth Dog Tests are an increasingly popular pastime for Russell owners, particularly in the US, where the Tests form part of an AKC-recognised sport. The purpose of the tests is to assess the dog's ability to go to ground and locate a quarry. The quarry is normally live rats, although artificial lures are also used occasionally. The rats are kept caged throughout the trial, as the dog's role is to locate the quarry not kill it.

In the US, the tests take place at AKC-approved venues, where an artificial tunnel has been dug. The AKC Earth Dog Tests have four, progressively difficult levels – Introductory, Junior, Senior, and Master, and the time allowed for the dog to reach his target varies according to the level at which he is being tested.

In the UK, the Kennel Club does not run its own Tests, but there are local Earth Dog Clubs for owners interested in pursuing this sport with their dogs.

RACING

If you thought racing was only for sighthounds – Greyhounds, Whippets and Lurchers – think again! Racing Russells is becoming an increasingly popular sport, particularly in the US. As with the more traditional racing breeds, Russells chase a lure around a racetrack, and the winner is the first to cross the finish line.

Terrier racing is taking off as a canine sport in the US.

THE SHOW DOG

Dog showing can be extremely rewarding, and it is a great way to meet new friends and engage in an active social scene with like-minded people.

For professional breeders, whose goal is to produce dogs of excellent 'type' (i.e. top-quality dogs conforming closely to the Breed Standard or blueprint of the 'ideal' dog), shows provide the opportunity for their dogs' merits to be assessed and recognised. Other people, such as the enthusiastic pet owner, may enter dog shows simply for fun.

If showing appeals to you, you should first think about the costs involved, which can be considerable. Entry fees and travelling expenses quickly mount up. So, unless you have a Russell of reasonable quality, you may find yourself spending an awful lot of money for very little reward.

THE BREED STANDARD

Every national kennel club has its own Breed Standard for each breed. The Breed Standard given below amalgamates the AKC Jack Russell Standard and the KC's Parson Russell Standard – the dogs are the same breed despite the different names.

GENERAL APPEARANCE

The Russell is a well-balanced dog, medium in size and bone, giving an impression of strength and endurance.

The Russell is a well-balanced dog which gives an impression of strength and endurance.

He has a harsh, weatherproof coat, which may be broken or smooth. His small, flexible chest enables him to pursue his quarry underground, while he has sufficient length of leg to follow the hounds. Any scars or injuries, which are the result of honourable work or accident, should not prejudice his chance in the show ring.

TEMPERAMENT AND CHARACTERISTICS

Workmanlike, active, and agile, he has an alert and confident character. Bold and friendly, he is tenacious and courageous at work. At home he is playful, exuberant and overwhelmingly affectionate. He requires his fair share of attention, but should never display shyness or aggression towards other dogs or people.

THE HEAD

The head is in proportion to the rest of the body, so that the appearance of balance is maintained. It is moderately broad, gradually narrowing as it reaches the eyes. The stop (the step-up from muzzle to skull) is well defined but shallow, and the length from stop to nose should be slightly shorter than from stop to occiput (the upper, back point of skull). The nose must be black and fully pigmented.

The typical expression is keen, and full of intelligence.

EYES: Almond-shaped, fairly deep-set, and dark in colour. Dark rims are desirable. The Russell's characteristic expression is keen, direct, and full of life and intelligence.

EARS: Button ear; small V-shaped ears, of moderate thickness, carried forward close to the head. The tip covers the orifice and points toward the eye. The fold is level, or slightly above, the top of the skull. When alert, tips do not extend below the corner of the eye.

DENTITION: The jaws are strong and muscular. Teeth are large with complete dentition in a perfect scissor bite, i.e. upper teeth closely overlapping the lower teeth and teeth set square to the jaws. Any deviation from this is a fault.

NECK: Clean, muscular, moderately arched, and of good length, gradually widening to the shoulders.

BODY

Well balanced and in proportion, so that the dog appears roughly square. The chest is narrow and of moderate depth, giving an athletic appearance. It must be capable of being spanned by moderate-sized hands. The ribs are fairly well sprung, oval rather than round, and should not extend past the level of the elbow.

The topline is strong, straight, and level in motion, with the loin slightly arched. The back is neither short nor long. The back gives no appearance of slackness but is laterally flexible, so that the dog may turn around in an earth.

TAIL: Set high and carried gaily, but not over the back or curled. Customarily docked so the tip is level to the skull, providing a good handhold. The tail must not be set low or carried over the back, i.e. squirrel tail. In the UK, undocked dogs can be shown – the tail should be of moderate length, straight, and give balance.

FOREQUARTERS: Long, sloping shoulders, well laid back, cleanly cut at the withers. The shoulder blade and upper arm are of approximately the same length, with the forelegs placed well under the dog. The elbows hang perpendicular to the body, working free of the sides. The legs are strong and straight, with good bone. The pasterns are firm and nearly straight.

HINDQUARTERS: Strong and muscular, smoothly moulded, with good angulation and bend of stifle (the joint of the hindleg between the thigh and the second thigh – the dog's knee). The hocks (joint on the hindleg) are short and parallel, with a driving action.

FEET: Round, cat-like, very compact, with thick and tough pads. The toes are moderately arched and pointing forward, turned neither in nor out. Hare feet are considered a major fault.

GAIT: The Russell's movement is free, lively, well co-ordinated, with straight action in front and behind. There should be ample reach and drive, with a good length of stride.

COLOUR: Entirely white, or predominantly white with black or tan markings, or a combination of these (tri-color). Colours are clear. Markings are preferably confined to the head and the root of the tail. Grizzle is acceptable and should not be confused with brindle, which is a disqualification.

Ideally, markings are confined to the head and the root of the tail.

The coat may be rough (pictured left), or smooth (pictured right).

COAT: Hair may be rough or smooth. Both types are harsh, close and dense; double-coated and weatherproof. The belly and undersides of the thighs are not bare. The dense undercoat is covered with a harsh, straight, tight jacket, which lies flat and close to the body and legs. There is a clear outline with only a hint of eyebrows and beard. The coat does not show a strong tendency to curl or wave.

SIZE, PROPORTION, SUBSTANCE

The ideal height is 33 cm (13 in) for bitches, and 35 cm (14 in) for dogs. The minimum heights are 30 cm (12 in) for bitches and 33 cm (13 in) for dogs. The AKC Standard states the ideal weight of a terrier in hard, working condition as between 13 to 17 lb (6 to 8 kg).

The judge's job is to assess each Russell against the Breed Standard.

SPANNING

Some Russell Standards carry a proviso about spanning. This is a measurement of the terrier's chest. The chest is spanned with hands tightly behind the elbows on the forward portion of the chest. The chest must be easily spanned by average-sized hands. The thumbs should meet at the spine, and the fingers should meet under the chest.

TESTICLES: Male animals should have two apparently normal testicles, fully descended into the scrotum.

IS MY DOG GOOD ENOUGH?

Before assessing your dog's physical attributes, you will need to be sure that his temperament is suited to showing. Your Russell must be confident and outgoing, and happy to be handled by the judge. If he displays any nervousness or aggression, he will be severely penalised in the show ring – no matter how good he looks.

To decide whether your dog looks good enough to enter the show scene, obtain a copy of the Breed Standard (available from your national kennel club or breed club). Cast a critical eye over your dog and compare him to the Standard. No dog will conform completely, as all dogs have some faults. Provided the faults are minor, however, this should not be any bar to competing successfully. If you are unsure about your dog's qualities, ask for the opinion of breed experts, either by attending a few shows or by joining your local breed club.

If your Russell conforms pretty well, dog showing may be the pastime for you. Remember, though, that your dog should first and foremost be a loved companion, and if he does not match the Breed Standard, it should not alter your feelings towards him.

The Russell must be trained to show himself off to full advantage.

SHOW TRAINING

Socialisation is the key to successful showing, and your Russell should be well socialised before he begins any show training. Joining your local breed club is an excellent starting point to develop further ring skills, as here your dog will become accustomed to being handled by several different people and having his teeth and – if applicable – his testicles checked.

If you decide to show, you will need a show collar and lead. Your breed club will advise you as to which are most suitable. You may also wish to join ring-training classes, where you will learn how to stand your dog in the show stance (so that his body is shown off to best advantage), and how to move him in the ring.

COLLECTABLES

If you want a less competitive hobby, you can join the growing band of Russell collectors.

There are books, paintings, postcards, porcelain and jewellery, which document the breed's history and show the Russell in all his moods. Beware! Once you start collecting, you will become a fanatic!

Your breed club may be a good place to start, as some have an extensive collection of clubware for sale. You may also find some interesting items in secondhand bookshops.

Collecting Russell memorabilia is a hobby that can soon take over your life.

The Healthy
Russell

The Russell is an intelligent, active breed. Due to their liveliness, Russells can be prone to accidents, but, in spite of this, they are one of the longest-lived breeds of dog – some reaching the age of twenty plus. This longevity makes the Russell prone to certain geriatric diseases. These and other common ailments are outlined below, along with a comprehensive programme of preventative health care to ensure your Russell stays in tip-top health.

PREVENTATIVE HEALTH CARE

It is better to prevent disease and maintain health than to be left in a situation where a disease runs its course and a cure cannot always be achieved. Regular checks with your veterinarian will allow specific advice to be given, as well as instituting preventative measures.

VACCINATIONS

There are a number of infectious conditions that dogs can be vaccinated against. These include the following:

BORDETELLA BRONCHISEPTICA: A bacterium that is part of

To begin with, puppies acquire immunity to disease from their mother's milk.

the infectious tracheitis (kennel cough) syndrome. This vaccine is administered by nasal drops to provide immunity. Kennel cough is an acute, usually self-limiting, infection of the upper respiratory tract.

In severe cases, especially where there is the involvement of canine distemper virus, it can lead to pneumonia. In small terriers, it is thought that kennel cough can lead to chronic bronchitis.

DISTEMPER: A viral disease causing discharges from the eyes and nose. Vomiting, diarrhoea and coughing may also occur. The virus in the skin causes thickening of the footpads (hard pad) and the nose. The virus also attacks the enamel of the teeth and can affect the nervous system, which may lead to convulsions.

The disease is spread by inhaling virus particles. Supportive care is the only treatment, and the condition is commonly fatal.

INFECTIOUS CANINE HEPATITIS: This is a viral condition that causes serious liver and kidney damage. It may also affect the eyes, causing clouding of the front of the eye.

Affected dogs mostly suffer acute vomiting. They are depressed, often off their food and may have a painful abdomen that can make them restless. Milder cases may only show slight lack of appetite before recovering. In severe cases, this condition is frequently fatal.

LEPTOSPIROSIS: This is a bacterial condition that attacks the kidneys and the liver. It is spread mainly through contact with contaminated water. Leptospirosis is commonly carried by rats and, as such, may pose an increased risk to Russells involved in hunting.

If the disease affects the kidneys, it may cause only vague signs. Affected dogs can become extremely depressed and show great thirst. They may also vomit and have a painful abdomen due to swelling of the kidneys. If the liver is affected, there is usually a sudden fever with jaundice. Dogs may also have an increased thirst, vomiting, plus blood-tinged diarrhoea.

Death can occur suddenly, or the condition can deteriorate quickly over a few days.

Leptospira bacteria are susceptible to many antibiotics, but, in the rapid liver form of the disease, treatment still may not be successful and so vaccination is advised.

PARAINFLUENZA: One of the viruses that can be involved in the kennel cough syndrome. It is thought to be of more importance in the United States where it can cause a nasal discharge and coughing. In the United Kingdom, it is more usually found together with other infectious agents.

The timing of vaccinations may vary, depending on the incidence of disease in your area.

PARVOVIRUS: A serious viral infection of the alimentary (digestive) tract, associated with acute vomiting and diarrhoea, as the virus attacks the ailmentary system. Blood is commonly found in both the vomit and diarrhoea.

Supportive treatment only can be given, and, in many cases, parvovirus infection results in death. In younger animals that recover, heart disease may be seen later in life due to virus particles damaging the heart.

RABIES: This is a viral disease of the nervous system. The virus is capable of infecting all mammals, including man, and when the disease runs its full course it is invariably fatal. It causes an encephalitis, which produces behavioural changes, including aggression, that assist in the transmission of the disease.

There are two main forms of the disease. The dumb form is the most common type in dogs. It causes a progressive paralysis of the muscles, which eventually leads to coma and death. The furious form is less common and is seen as restlessness and irritability. Some dogs with the furious form will die during a severe seizure, but in most (as in the dumb form) paralysis of the muscles develops.

The UK has been free of rabies due to quarantine regulations, and this status is being maintained with a new policy of vaccination for those animals entering or re-entering the country. The vaccination is carried out in conjunction with identification, using a unique microchip number. It also relies on blood-testing to confirm that immunity has been developed in the animal vaccinated.

The virus maintains itself mainly in the wild animal population (e.g. via foxes, skunks and raccoons).

VACCINE REGIMES

A vaccination regime against infectious diseases should be discussed with your veterinarian, so that it can be individually tailored after an assessment of the risk of contracting these diseases. Generally, pups in an at-risk area require two vaccinations to produce an effective immune response against these diseases.

The timing of these vaccines depends on the immune status of the dam, and the relative risk in the local area. The bitch will, if vaccinated, produce colostrum, which will confer some immunity against these diseases to her offspring.

The pup's vaccination is usually performed when this immunity is wearing off, usually at around 8-12 weeks of age. In some high-risk areas, vaccination may be performed as early as 6 weeks of age.

In order to maintain immunity against these diseases, booster vaccinations are required during adulthood. Again, these should be individually tailored according to the individual risk. The health checks usually performed at the time of vaccination also enable your veterinarian to possibly identify diseases in their early stages and so take early action to protect your pet's health.

EXTERNAL PARASITES

FLEAS

These are an extremely common parasite of the dog. There are many species of flea that can live on dogs, but all cause similar signs. In mild cases, this is confined to scratching, ranging to severe hair loss and skin infection in more serious infestations. In very young animals, the blood loss caused by fleas feeding can result in a severe anaemia. Fleas also have a role in the spread of tapeworms in dogs.

There are many products now available, which provide safe and very effective flea

Routine treatment is required to prevent flea infestation.

prevention. Ask your vet to recommend a suitable treatment. With the advent of central heating in most homes, your dog will need year-round protection. Working Russells are more prone to fleas due to contact with wildlife.

LICE

There are two types of lice: those that suck blood, and those that feed on skin and hair debris. They are an occasional parasite of dogs, commonly causing scratching. Lice and their eggs are visible to the naked eye when the coat is parted. Again, there are a number of effective treatments.

MITES

There are several types of mite causing different types of infection, more broadly known as mange. The signs can vary from hair loss with no other symptoms to severe and intense itching. Mites are not visible to the naked eye and may be diagnosed on skin scrapings or blood serology tests. Again, working terriers may be more susceptible due to contact with infected wild animals. Sarcoptic mites may cause lesions on people.

TICKS

Ticks may cause local skin reactions, and, in severe cases, significant blood loss. Importantly, ticks may carry and spread other infectious diseases caused by bacteria, protozoans and viruses.

Lyme disease is one of these bacterial diseases. It is endemic in north-eastern America and has also been reported in Europe. When this bacterium is injected by a tick into a dog, then lameness and a fever usually result. The lameness is caused by arthritis. The bacteria

A spot-on application will give all-round protection.

is sensitive to antibiotics; however, long courses of treatment are required, and diagnosis can be difficult. Lyme disease is a zoonotic disease and so can spread to people handling infected urine and blood. The signs in people are similar to dogs, but humans can also develop meningitis and encephalitis.

The best prevention for Lyme disease is regular tick treatment. The bacteria that causes Lyme disease is not injected straight away by the tick and so effective tick treatments will prevent this disease.

INTERNAL PARASITES

TAPEWORMS

These parasites live in the intestines. They are flat and segmented; segments may be seen in the faeces of infected dogs. The life cycle of tapeworms usually involves other animals as an intermediate host. The lifestyle of many Russells predisposes them to tapeworm infection, especially those that scavenge and hunt.

ROUNDWORMS

There are several different species of roundworm, with differing lifestyles, affecting different parts of the dog.

Intestinal roundworms, like tapeworms, live in the alimentary system and may cause diarrhoea or constipation, vomiting, and may lead to weight loss and lack of condition.

Lungworms – these move through the alimentary tract and the lungs, and may result in coughing and pneumonia as well as the intestinal signs mentioned above. Damage done to the lung may be permanent and may contribute to development of bronchitis.

Heartworm – this worm lives in a dog's large pulmonary vessels and the heart. It is seen widely throughout the world, but in the UK it is seen only in some imported dogs. Symptoms are a chronic cough, weight loss and ultimately congestive heart failure. It is spread via biting mosquitoes and so is less common in cooler climates. Treatment is mainly aimed at prevention, because, once infected, treatment can be hazardous.

TREATMENT

Regular worming with broad-spectrum treatments is advised. This should be carried out more frequently in working dogs who may pick up large worm burdens from their prey.

Routine worming is not only advised for animal health reasons but also to safeguard human health. Some types of worm, in particular, *Toxocara* and *Echinococcus* worms, may cause serious health problems in people, especially children.

DENTISTRY

Dental disease is a common problem in all dogs. It poses more problems as animals age, and, because the Russell is a long-lived breed, individuals are commonly treated for dental disorders. Hunting and working Russells are prone to traumatic dental disorders that include fractured teeth and torn gums. However, more

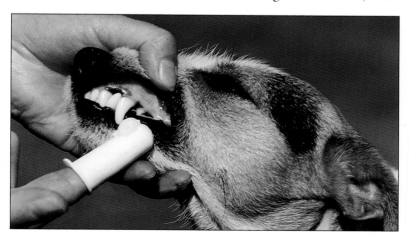

Regular brushing will keep the teeth clean and the gums healthy.

commonly, periodontal disease is seen following plaque and tartar build-up. This leads to gum disease and recession, and eventually to the loss of the teeth.

The gums possess a very good blood supply; when the gums are infected, this blood supply spreads infection more widely around the body, particularly to the liver, kidneys, lungs and heart.

Preventative measures can be very successful; brushing the teeth in compliant individuals is the most effective. Other methods include the use of hard chews, dry diets and oral gels. The success of all these methods relies on the frequency with which they are administered.

Regular dental checks by your veterinarian will allow early identification of dental and gum disease prior to irreversible changes such as tooth loss.

OBESITY

This is a problem that becomes more evident with age as dogs become less active. It exacerbates other pre-existing diseases including arthritis, heart disease and diabetes. It is wholly preventable by monitoring weight regularly and, if required, adjusting the food intake accordingly.

A-Z OF COMMON AILMENTS

ARTHRITIS

This is a degenerative disease of the joints, which becomes more common as the dog ages. It will also occur in younger, active dogs that have had previous joint problems.

It is characterised by stiffness of the affected joint and often pain. Dogs may be lame and show a reluctance to exercise. X-rays of the affected joint may show extra bone formation around the joint. This extra bone, and damage to cartilage within the joint, make the disease painful and limit the mobility of the joint.

Treatment is aimed at reducing pain and preventing further degeneration. Exercise must be controlled, the dog's weight should be monitored, and physiotherapy may be of benefit to certain individuals. However, usually, the disease progresses slowly, in spite of treatment, and will lead to eventual joint failure.

BRONCHITIS

In common with other small terriers, lower airway disease (bronchitis) occurs occasionally, usually in middle-aged to older dogs. It is a non-specific inflammation of the lower airways and lungs, which results in a long-standing cough.

The cause of the disease is usually not known, but an infectious disease such as kennel cough may make some dogs more prone. Other factors which may be implicated in the disease are environmental pollution, including cigarette smoke, and possible allergic reactions. It is a difficult condition to diagnose and treat. Your vet may advise X-rays and other tests to aid diagnosis.

In the long term, bronchitis will cause an irritating cough, wheezing, and difficulty in breathing. Affected individuals may also tire easily. They are also predisposed to recurrent bouts of pneumonia. Treatment is aimed at controlling the signs of the

Bronchitis commonly affects small breeds of terrier.

disease, easing the breathing, and reducing the cough. Once again, obesity can exacerbate this condition.

CATARACT

Cataracts are dense opacities of the lens of the eye, usually caused by an upset to the metabolism of the lens. In Russells, traumatic cataracts occur following either a blunt or penetrating injury to the eye. Cataracts will also form as a result of diabetes (see below).

Treatment for cataracts is usually surgical removal of the affected lens after confirmation that the structures behind the cataract have not been damaged. If cataracts are not treated, progressive blindness will result. Depending on the individual dog, this may be tolerated surprisingly well.

CUSHING'S SYNDROME (HYPERADRENOCORTICISM)

This is a hormonal disease that results in the overproduction of steroid hormones from the adrenal glands. It occurs in middle-aged dogs. It is not uncommon in the Russell breed, and slightly more than half of the affected animals are bitches.

The main signs of the disease are an increase in appetite and thirst. Other symptoms include hair loss, skin thickening and thinning, a pot-bellied appearance, and muscle weakness. The dog may also develop symmetrical bald areas. Bitches may remain out of heat. Some dogs will also develop diabetes. Diagnosis can be difficult

Bitches are more commonly affected by Cushing's syndrome.

and will require a variety of investigations including blood tests and analysis of urine.

Treatment depends on the specific cause and may be medical or surgical. Medical therapy is lifelong, and will require regular monitoring so that the signs of overproduction of steroid hormones are not seen. Surgical treatment is often very difficult.

CRUCIATE LIGAMENT RUPTURE

The cruciate ligaments are crossing ligaments in the centre of the stifle (knee) joint. They provide forward and backward stability of the joint. This disease can occur at any age.

In younger animals, it tends to occur following sudden turning at a run, when the ligament is placed under extreme strain and will suddenly snap. In older animals, there can be gradual stretching or tearing of the ligament. If the dog is overweight, jumping up or down will rupture the ligament. This then causes instability of the joint, so that the dog is very lame.

A cruciate ligament rupture may occur following a sudden turn.

Some smaller dogs can be treated with rest, and the joint will tighten with time and increase in stability. Many dogs require surgery to improve the stability of the joint and the results can be very good.

However, arthritis can result in the affected joint, regardless of whether surgery was performed.

DIABETES MELLITUS (SUGAR DIABETES)

This disease is characterised by an increase in thirst and a ravenous appetite. It is usually diagnosed with blood and urine tests, looking for high glucose (sugar) levels in the blood and urine. These tests are also required in the ongoing monitoring of the disease.

Treatment depends on the type of diabetes. In some dogs, a change in diet is required. However, lifelong treatment with daily insulin injections is generally needed. Insulin is the hormone that regulates glucose levels. This disease also occurs more commonly in middle-aged, overweight dogs. In some cases of Cushing's syndrome (see above), diabetes will also occur as a complication.

In advanced cases of diabetes, dogs will show lack of appetite and vomiting, and there may be a smell of acetone on their breath. When diabetes occurs in bitches, spaying is often advised to prevent loss of stability due to fluctuations in the progestogen (a female sex hormone) levels that occur when the bitch is in season.

JUVENILE ATAXIA

This is thought to have a hereditary basis in the Russell breed. There are degenerative changes in the nerves of the spinal cord that cause a wobbly, almost drunken, gait. It is usually seen in quite young dogs.

LEGG-CALVE-PERTHES DISEASE

This is an extremely painful condition of the hips. It is usually seen in young dogs. Its cause is not known, and so no preventative advice can be given. It develops when the head of the femur (the 'ball' of the

*Patellar luxation is a common
condition in Russells.*

hip's ball and socket joint) loses its blood supply, and the bone dies. This leads to an uneven surface within the joint, which causes painful functioning of the joint. Treatment involves pain relief, but, in some cases, surgery to remove the affected hip joint may be required. Quite commonly, both hip joints can be affected.

PATELLAR LUXATION (DISLOCATING KNEECAPS)

This common condition affecting Russells occurs when the patella slips out of its normal groove when the leg bends. It is seen when dogs are walking, and they will occasionally skip or hop on their hindlimbs. Both hindlimbs can be affected in the same dog. There is variation in the severity of the condition, and, in some dogs, it does not appear to cause too many problems. In other dogs, it can be painful and debilitating.

Treatment is usually surgical, and can involve the veterinarian deepening the groove in which the patella sits. This is often in conjunction with altering the direction in which the patella is pulled, when the leg bends, by moving its attachment on the tibial bone.

All dogs with this condition will develop arthritis of the affected joint in time, and this will be treated as described above.

PRIMARY LENS LUXATION (PLL)

The lens within the eye is held in position by a ligament called the zonule. When this weakens, the lens loses support and can displace into either the front or back of the eye. If the lens displaces into the front of the eye, it will cause clouding of the cornea (the clear front part of the eye), and glaucoma will also develop. Glaucoma is an increased pressure within the eyeball, and can lead to blindness.

Treatment usually involves surgery on the affected lens. However, the condition usually affects both eyes, with one eye showing signs before the other. If diagnosed, careful observation of the unaffected eye is required.

Subluxation of the lens is a less severe form of the disease, when the displacement of the lens is not so great. Usually, the subluxated lens will develop into a cataract. It will always develop into a full luxation, but this can take many months or even years. However, a dog with a boisterous disposition will tend to hasten the process of luxation.

If the lens displaces into the back of the eye, it is less likely to cause problems, but it can always displace forwards in the future. Removal of the lens from the back of the eye is usually more difficult, and so the patient is observed for the lens moving forward, and lens removal is carried out when that occurs.

TRAUMATIC INJURIES

Traumatic injuries are frequently seen in the Russell because of their boisterous disposition. Skin tears and lacerations are common in working dogs. Prey and thorns can cause these. More serious injuries can be seen in cases where there is inter-dog aggression. The injuries will need individual assessment for their treatment.

SUMMARY

After reading about the ailments that can affect a Russell, you could be forgiven for thinking the breed is prone to ill health. Fortunately, this is very far from being the case. The Russell is a fit, active dog, built on workmanlike lines, and, given the correct care, your dog should live a long, happy and healthy life.

Further Information

KENNEL CLUBS

American Kennel Club
5580 Centerview Dr.
Raleigh, NC 27606
(919) 233-9767
www.akc.org

Kennel Club
1 Clarges Street, London
W1J 8AB
0870 606 6750
www.the-kennel-club.org.uk

HEALTH SCHEMES

**Canine Eye Registration
Foundation (CERF)**
1248 Lynn Hall
Purdue University
West Lafayette, IN 47907
(317) 494-8179
vet.purdue.edu/depts/prog/cerf.html

**Orthopedic Foundation for
Animals (OFA)**
2300 Nifong Blvd.
Columbia, MO 65201
www.offa.org

Synbiotics (PennHIP)
11011 Via Frontera
San Diego, CA 92127

BVA/KC schemes
Contact either the Kennel Club,
above (click on the health pages of
the website) or get in touch with
the BVA.
British Veterinary Association
7 Mansfield Street
London W1G 9NQ
www.bva.co.uk
0207 636 6541

BREED ORGANISATIONS

**Jack Russell Terrier Club of
America, Inc.**
P.O. Box 4527
Lutherville, MD 21094-4527
(410) 561-3655

**The Jack Russell Terrier
Association of America**
(formerly the Jack Russell Breeders'
Association)
P.O. Box 115
Winchester Center, CT 06094
(203) 379-3282

**The Parson Russell
Terrier Club**
Mrs Ruth Hussey-Wilford
Pirton House, Pirton
Worcester, WR8 9EJ
01905 821440